Cambridge English Readers

Level 1

Series editor: Philip Prowse

Hotel Casanova

Sue Leather

CAMBRIDGE
UNIVERSITY PRESS

CAMBRIDGE
UNIVERSITY PRESS

University Printing House, Cambridge CB2 8BS, United Kingdom

One Liberty Plaza, 20th Floor, New York, NY 10006, USA

477 Williamstown Road, Port Melbourne, VIC 3207, Australia

314–321, 3rd Floor, Plot 3, Splendor Forum, Jasola District Centre,
New Delhi – 110025, India

79 Anson Road, #06–04/06, Singapore 079906

Cambridge University Press is part of the University of Cambridge.

It furthers the University's mission by disseminating knowledge in the pursuit of
education, learning and research at the highest international levels of excellence.

www.cambridge.org
Information on this title: www.cambridge.org/9780521649971

First published 2005

Printed in Great Britain by Ashford Colour Press Ltd.

Illustrations by Hannah Webb

A catalogue record for this publication is available from the British Library

ISBN 978-0-521-64997-1 Paperback

Contents

People in the story

Dino Bracco: A young man who works at the Hotel Grand in Venice.

Carla Maretti: A woman who comes to the hotel.

Maria Luca: A waitress at the hotel.

Giovanni Tardelli: Dino's boss.

Beppo Rossi: A young man who works with Dino at the Hotel Grand.

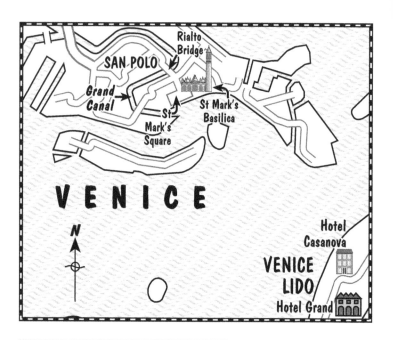

RialtoBridge

SAN POLO

Grand Canal

St Mark's Square

St Mark's Basilica

VENICE

N

Hotel Casanova

VENICE LIDO

Hotel Grand

Venice

ITALY

Rome

N

Roccella

Chapter 1   *Dino*

20 April was Dino Bracco's twenty-first birthday. He worked. Giovanni, his boss at the Hotel Grand, brought him a cake from the hotel kitchen. 'Just twenty-one!' said Giovanni, and he put his hand on Dino's back. 'Ah, Dino, Dino . . . when I was twenty-one . . . !'

Dino ate some cake and smiled. He was only twenty-one years old, but he was a young man who knew what he wanted. He had a plan.

'You must know what you want, Dino,' his mother said to him when he was a child. And he did. He had a plan. Dino came from a very small town called Roccella, in the south of Italy. His mother and father were farmers. Roccella was beautiful but no-one had any money. Dino was born there, but now he lived and worked in Venice. He worked at the reception of the Hotel Grand.

'Wow!' said Dino's friends in Roccella. 'You're at a big hotel on the Venice Lido. How did you get that job?'

Dino smiled. 'Because I work hard,' he thought, 'and I have a plan.'

Dino liked his work at the reception. When guests came in, he said hello to them and he asked, 'Sir, madam, would you like a glass of Soave, one of Venice's famous wines?' He took their credit cards. When they weren't from Italy, he took their passports. Then he asked the boy to take their bags to their room. He helped the guests. 'Yes, madam, of course, madam.' Dino's boss, Giovanni Tardelli, thought he was a good boy.

He knew a girl at the hotel who also came from Roccella. Her name was Maria Luca and she worked as a waitress. Maria was nice and he liked to talk to her, but she was just a friend. On his birthday, she gave him a small picture of Roccella, their town.

'I did it,' she smiled at him. 'You can look at the picture and think about home.'

'Thank you, Maria!' Dino smiled and put the picture in his little room. The picture was nice, but he didn't think about Roccella much. He liked to think about his plans.

Women liked Dino. Well, why not? He was good-looking, with dark curly hair and beautiful brown eyes. And he was nice. The women who came to the hotel liked to talk to him. Dino was kind to them. But women were not in Dino's plans. Not for the moment. 'When I'm twenty-six,' he thought, 'I'm going to meet a woman, the woman I want to marry.'

Dino knew that it was important to look good. It was his job. He always wore good clothes: beautiful shirts, nice jackets and trousers. His hair always looked good and he was always *elegante*. He knew that Italy was famous for nice clothes and beautiful things. That's why people came to Italy, to Venice.

Dino worked very long hours and he didn't make much money. His room at the back of the hotel was very small. It just had a small bed, a table and light, and somewhere for his clothes.

But Dino didn't think about the long hours, the little money and the small room. He liked his job at the Hotel Grand. And it was only the start. He knew what he wanted. Every night he wrote about the day in his little black book. Then he looked at his plans. He liked to read them every day.

The night of 20 April, his twenty-first birthday, Dino sat in his little room and looked at his little black book. He looked at his plans. 'Everything is good,' he thought. But on 21 April, something changed his plans. The woman with the long dark hair came and stayed at the Hotel Grand, and everything changed.

Chapter 2 *Dino in love*

'Good morning. My name is Carla Maretti,' said the woman, 'and I have a room.'

Dino looked up from his computer. The woman was talking to Beppo, the other young man who worked at the reception. Dino saw a beautiful woman with brown eyes. She smiled and looked into Dino's eyes. He looked down quickly, but it was too late.

The woman left the reception to go to her room. Again, Dino looked up. The woman was very slim, and she wore a beautiful blue jacket. It was the colour of the sky in spring and it looked very expensive.

'Do you like her?' asked Beppo, laughing.

Dino looked down again quickly. 'No, I . . . er . . . I'm just trying to finish this . . .'

Beppo laughed again and went into the kitchen.

That evening, Dino was in reception. At about eleven thirty, he heard the telephone. He looked at the room lights. It was Room 216. Carla Maretti's room. He answered the phone. 'Reception, can I help you, madam?'

'Yes,' said the beautiful voice. 'I want a sandwich, but Room Service is not replying.'

'I can help you, madam,' said Dino. Dino phoned Room Service and asked them to phone Room 216. About forty-five minutes later, the woman in Room 216 phoned Reception again.

'I just want to say thank you,' said Carla Maretti, 'and you have a very nice voice.'

Dino's face went red. They talked for a minute or two. She lived in Rome, but she loved Venice. He told her that his name was Dino. They laughed. He thought she was very nice.

The next day, Dino thought about Carla Maretti all the time. At about four thirty in the afternoon, she came into the hotel. She had lots of bags from expensive shops. She looked tired after her day of shopping. She went into the café just across from the reception.

Dino walked quickly into the café. Carla Maretti asked for a coffee. Dino walked up to the young waiter, took the coffee and said, 'Can I take that?' The waiter smiled at Dino.

'Your coffee, madam,' said Dino. He put the small cup of coffee in front of Carla Maretti. She looked up.

'It's the man with the beautiful voice – Dino,' she said. She looked at him, and he looked into her brown eyes.

'Er . . . your coffee, madam,' he smiled.

He turned to go, but she took his arm. She pulled him to her until his ear was near her mouth.

11

'This evening, at about ten thirty,' she said, 'I'm going to order drinks in my room. Please bring them. Do you understand?'

Dino went red. 'Er, I . . . well, yes, madam,' he said.

'Very good,' she said. She picked up the *Corriere della Sera* newspaper and started to read it.

Dino went back to the reception and waited. He phoned Room Service. 'When Room 216 orders drinks,' he said, 'I want to take them to Signora Maretti's room.'

Time went very slowly. Then, at about ten thirty, Room Service phoned. Dino took Carla Maretti's drinks to her room.

'Ah, the man with the beautiful voice,' she said when she opened the door. 'Come in. I want to talk to you.'

Carla drank whisky. Dino drank water, because he was still at work.

'Sit down here,' said Carla, 'and tell me everything about yourself.'

Dino never told anyone about his plans, but he told Carla. He talked to her about his plan to marry when he was twenty-six. 'And then, when I'm thirty years old, I want my own hotel, with my name over the door,' he said. 'I want it more than anything in the world.'

Carla listened. Her eyes didn't leave Dino's face. His face was red. He felt hot. 'Hotel Casanova,' he finished.

'How wonderful,' she said, 'Hotel Casanova! What a beautiful plan . . . and you are very nice.' She put her hand on his hot face and pulled him towards her. She kissed him. He kissed her. Dino kissed girls back home in Roccella. But their kisses weren't like Carla's kisses.

That night Dino didn't sleep in his little room. He slept

with Carla Maretti in Room 216. At five o'clock in the morning, Dino opened his eyes. 'Oh, no!' he thought. 'I'm in love. I'm not twenty-six. I'm just twenty-one years old and I'm in love!'

Chapter 3 *'I'm yours!'*

Dino turned over and kissed Carla on her head and she opened her eyes. 'My love,' she said, and put her arms around him.

'I must go,' he said in her ear. 'Oh no,' he thought, 'I'm in a guest's room. What about my plans? This is *not* in my plans.' But he felt very good.

'Me too,' she said. 'I must go to Rome for a day or two.'

'Really?' asked Dino.

'Yes, darling,' she said, 'but I'll come back.'

Dino put on his clothes and kissed Carla. 'I love you,' he said to her.

Carla smiled. 'And I love you too, darling,' she said.

Dino went back to his work and Carla went back to Rome. It was a good thing, thought Dino. He needed time to think. He was in love!

For the next two or three days, Dino thought about Carla all the time. Three days after Carla went to Rome, Dino had a day off work. He went to the centre of Venice. From the Hotel Grand there was a boat to the centre. The boat, the *vaporetto*, took you across the water to St Mark's, right in the centre of the city. Dino thought it was the most beautiful city in the world. When he had a day off, he liked to walk in the city.

Dino walked by the famous canals and the beautiful old houses. The spring day was warm. He went to sit and have coffee in St Mark's square. He liked to do this sometimes. He thought it was the *only* place in Venice to drink coffee.

Dino ordered coffee and watched the people in the square. There were lots of people from all over the world. Dino saw some young lovers. They kissed and they looked very happy. Oh, where was Carla? He thought about Carla all the time. He loved her, and she loved him.

Dino drank his coffee and got up. Then he walked across the famous old Rialto Bridge and into San Polo. Then he went down the little streets, and watched the gondolas on the smaller canals. He always loved to watch the black gondolas and the gondoliers. Dino thought about Carla. He wanted to enjoy Venice with her. Carla, Carla . . .

He turned back to the Grand Canal. This was the most important canal in Venice. He watched a gondola come out of a small canal into the Grand Canal. Then a motor boat came down the Grand Canal. It was very fast. Dino watched. Was the fast motor boat going to crash into the slow gondola? No, it was OK. They didn't crash. But there were a lot of crashes in Venice, thought Dino, because there were lots of boats on the water. Dino walked to the *vaporetto* and went back to the Hotel Grand.

Two days later Dino had a telephone call from Carla.

'*Amore*, it's me.' Carla called him 'love'. Dino felt happy.

'Carla!' he said, 'where are you? I'm thinking about you all the time . . .'

'It's OK, my love,' said Carla, 'I'm here in Rome.'

'I love you,' said Dino.

'I love you too, *amore*,' said Carla. 'Dino . . . ?'

'Yes?'

'Why don't we get married?' asked Carla. 'You love me and I love you. I have a lot of money and I can buy your Hotel Casanova for you!'

Dino listened and thought. He was only twenty-one. His plan was to have the hotel when he was thirty years old. But why not have it now? His plan was to get married when he was twenty-six. But why not get married now? He loved Carla and she loved him. She wasn't twenty-one, but she was very rich. And he loved her . . . But he loved her because of *her*, not because of her money. Sometimes you must take what life gives you. His mother always said that.

'Yes!' said Dino.

'My love,' said Carla, 'I'm yours!'

Chapter 4   *'You're mine!'*

In June, Dino married Carla. Two months later, they found a beautiful hotel on the Venice Lido. It was next to the water. Carla bought it for Dino, and Dino called it 'Hotel Casanova.' He bought new furniture and found waiters and people to work at the hotel. Dino had everything he wanted: he had Carla and he had his Hotel Casanova. And he was only twenty-one!

Dino worked a lot in August, September and October. There were lots of people at the hotel. He worked day and night. He didn't leave the hotel. Then one day in November, he felt very tired. 'I'm going to take a week off, my love,' he said to Carla. 'I must go to Milan to see someone about the furniture for the restaurant.'

'No,' said Carla. 'You can't go without me . . .'

'But, my love,' said Dino, with his hand on her arm, 'I need to get away for a day or two. You know I'm very tired.'

Carla walked away from her husband. 'I said NO,' she shouted.

Dino looked at her. 'She's just tired too,' he thought. 'It isn't important. I can stay here.'

But over the next two or three months, Carla didn't change. Every time he tried to leave the hotel without her, she said 'No.'

'What is it?' he asked her one day. 'Why can't I go away without you?'

'I'm afraid. Are you going to meet a new woman?' she said. 'Are you going to leave me, because you have your hotel now?'

Dino laughed. '*Amore*, why do you think that? I love you. I don't want to leave you.'

Dino waited, but nothing changed. He began to feel very bad. 'I can't go out,' he thought. 'I can't do anything without Carla. I just work at the hotel every day.'

One morning, Dino felt very unhappy. It was one year and three months after they got married. 'I must get out of here,' he thought.

'I must leave,' Dino said to Carla. 'I don't want this. You

say that I can't go out without you. I just work at the hotel. I'm not happy.'

'You can never leave me! You're mine!' Carla looked at him. Her eyes were very angry.

'Yes, I can,' said Dino. But he felt afraid.

'Go!' said Carla. 'Go – and I can tell everyone about Alessandro . . . that you and I killed him!'

Dino turned quickly and looked at Carla. 'What are you talking about?'

'Alessandro, my husband!' she shouted. 'Don't tell me that you don't know!'

'She isn't well,' thought Dino. 'What are you talking about?' he asked her again.

'You and me!' she said. 'We planned to kill Alessandro! It was your plan. You said, "Kill him on the road to Sorrento," and I did it. The police thought it was a road accident. I did it, but it was your plan!'

'But . . .'

'And that's why you've got your hotel!' she said. 'Alessandro's money! It bought you the hotel.'

Dino felt cold.

'Try and leave me!' She laughed. 'And I tell the police *everything*.'

Dino looked at her with his mouth open. 'What can I say? The police are going to think that Carla and I killed her husband!' he thought.

Dino went to bed, but he didn't sleep. All night he thought about Carla's words. Was it all true? He thought about when he met Carla at the Hotel Grand. He thought about the week when she went to Rome. He thought about when she phoned him and said, 'We can get married.' Dino didn't know anything about Alessandro; he didn't know that she had a husband. He never asked!

Dino's mother often said, 'We just see what we want to see.' Well, that was true, he thought.

'Carla killed her husband,' thought Dino. 'Am I next?' Dino thought again about what Carla said: 'You can never leave me! You're mine!'

Chapter 5 *The girl from Roccella*

The next morning, Dino went to his office and closed the door. He turned on his computer. He found the name 'Alessandro Maretti' on the internet.

'Millionaire dies in accident on road to Sorrento.' Dino looked at his computer and read: '1 May'. That was when Carla went to Rome! But she was with Alessandro, her husband. It was true! There was Carla's name! She was in the car with Alessandro! Everyone thought it was an accident, but he died and she didn't. And she got all his money.

What was he going to do? Carla was crazy! She killed her first husband – was Dino next?

'I must think,' he said, 'and I mustn't do anything stupid.'

Dino started work. He felt very bad, but he worked. But he thought about Carla a lot. 'Who can I tell?' he thought. What about Giovanni? That was a good plan! He phoned the Hotel Grand, but his old boss wasn't there. Dino didn't know what to do.

A week went by. Dino needed some new waiters and waitresses for the Hotel Casanova. He sat at his desk and talked to a lot of men and women. Now it was five o'clock in the afternoon and the last person was at his door.

'Come in!' he called.

A pretty young woman walked in.

'Maria!' Dino said. 'How wonderful to see you!'

It was Maria Luca, the girl from Roccella! The girl who worked with him at the Hotel Grand. The girl who gave him the picture for his birthday.

'I'm very happy to see you!' Dino said. He stood up and gave her a chair. 'Sit down here. How are things at the Hotel Grand? How is Giovanni? Would you like a coffee?'

A waiter brought some coffee, and the two friends talked. They talked about the people they knew and about the Hotel Casanova. Dino forgot about Carla.

'I heard about your hotel,' said Maria, 'and I want to work with you again. The Hotel Grand is nice, but this is beautiful! I'd love to be a waitress here!'

Dino knew that Maria was a very good waitress. She was nice to the guests, and she was also intelligent.

'Listen,' he said, 'I'm happy to give you a job, but I need

someone to be the boss of all my waiters and waitresses.'
Dino smiled at Maria and said, 'I'd like *you* to do it!'

After that, Maria went to work at the Hotel Casanova.
Dino saw her every day, and every day he liked her more
and more. She was very sweet and kind. They talked a lot
and they were good friends. When he was with her, he
didn't think about Carla.

But Carla saw everything.

'You like that girl!' she said one evening. 'You like her too much!'

'I don't know what you're talking about,' said Dino.

'Yes, you do,' said Carla. 'Think, Dino. You are my husband! You're mine!'

Dino found the little picture of Roccella that Maria gave him on his birthday. He put it on the wall of his office. He looked at it every day. It was true, thought Dino, that he was in love with Maria. She was sweet and good. Like Roccella. And he knew that Maria loved him too. She didn't say anything. After all, Dino was married to Carla. But he knew.

'I killed Alessandro and I can kill you too!' continued Carla. 'Don't forget that, Dino!'

'She's crazy,' Dino thought. Then he knew what to do. He went to Maria that evening. 'We must leave the hotel, you and I. I can't tell you why now, but I can tell you when we get out of the hotel.'

'But . . .'

'I can't tell you now. Come on!'

Dino took Maria by the hand and they went out of a back door, down to the water. It was a dark November evening. There were boats there. 'Take us to the Grand Canal!' he said to the boatman.

Dino and Maria didn't see Carla. But Carla watched them from the window. She ran out quickly and took the fast hotel boat. 'She can't have him,' she said. 'He's mine!'

Chapter 6 *On a gondola*

On the boat, Dino told Maria everything. Maria's eyes got bigger and bigger. But she knew Dino. He was from Roccella. She knew that he was a good man. And she loved him. She loved him when they worked at the Hotel Grand.

'And now I know all about her – she's a killer!' said Dino.

Dino looked into Maria's eyes. He didn't see Carla behind them in the fast hotel boat.

All across the water to Venice, Carla's boat got closer. Then it was just a hundred metres behind them.

'At the Grand Canal, we can get a gondola,' Dino said to Maria.

That night, there were a lot of boats. 'Gondola!' shouted Dino and a black gondola came up to them. They got in and went up the Grand Canal. Dino smiled. He was with Maria in the most beautiful city in the world.

Carla saw Dino and Maria in the gondola and she was very angry. She saw that they were in love. 'He's mine!' Carla shouted. Carla's fast boat went onto the Grand Canal, after Dino and Maria's gondola. 'I'm going to kill them!' she said.

But just then a red fireboat came down a small canal. The blue light on top of the fireboat was flashing. The fireboat was very fast. It came out into the Grand Canal and went into Carla's hotel boat. It was all very quick. There was a big noise. Carla and the hotel boat went down into the dirty waters of the Grand Canal.

'I love you,' said Dino to Maria, 'and I want to be with you always.'

'I love you too,' said Maria.

Dino and Maria heard the noise behind them, but they didn't look back.

Cambridge English Readers

Look out for other titles in the series:

Level 1

Next Door to Love
by Margaret Johnson

'You need to meet new people, Stella,' my best friend often told me. 'New men.' But I didn't want to meet new men, and I didn't want a boyfriend. Then Tony arrived next door and everything changed.

The Big Picture
by Sue Leather

Ken Harada takes photos for newspapers. But life gets dangerous when Ken takes a photo of a sumo star. Someone wants the photo badly. But who? And why?

Bad Love
by Sue Leather

'Dr. Jack Daly?' Judy said. 'He's famous.' 'I don't often like famous people,' I said. 'Oh, come on, Detective Laine!'

One week later Daly is dead and Flick Laine is looking for his killer.

Just Like a Movie
by Sue Leather

Brad Black and his girlfriend Gina like the movies. They are happy, but they have no money. Then Brad has an idea and thinks that real life can be just like the movies – and that's when things go wrong.

Blood Diamonds
by Richard MacAndrew

Van Delft is a businessman. He buys and sells things in many countries. But some people think he also buys and sells guns and diamonds.

Kirkpatrick and Shepherd are two journalists. They are writing a front-page story – about blood diamonds. Is Van Delft the man they want?

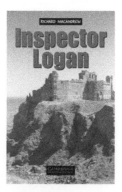

Inspector Logan
by Richard MacAndrew

'When did your wife go out?' asked Jenny Logan.

'Yesterday,' the man replied.

'And she didn't come home last night?'

'That's right,' said the man.

It was Jenny Logan's first day as a police inspector. This was her first murder.

Parallel
by Colin Campbell

'Max sat on his bed. There was a gun on the bed beside him. The gun was still warm.'

Max kills people for money. But one day he goes to a new world and his life changes.

Help!
by Philip Prowse

Frank Wormold is a writer. To help him finish one of his stories, he starts to use a computer. But the computer gives him more help than he wants.

Level 2

Within High Fences
by Penny Hancock

'There was nothing different about that night. But that night, my life started to change.'

It's the night when Nancy meets George. But it isn't easy for them to be together. There's Nancy's job and her boyfriend. And will George have to return to his own country?

Jojo's Story
by Antoinette Moses

'There aren't any more days. There's just time. Time when it's dark and time when it's light. Everything is dead, so why not days too?'

Everyone in Jojo's village is dead, and ten-year-old Jojo is alone.

Different Worlds
by Margaret Johnson

'In my world there are no birds singing. There are no noisy men working on the roads. No babies crying.'

Sam is like any other teenage girl except that she is deaf. Now she is in love with Jim, but are their worlds too different?

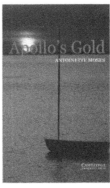

Apollo's Gold
by Antoinette Moses

Liz studies and teaches archaeology in Athens. She goes on holiday to the beautiful island of Sifnos. But one of the local men dies, and Liz becomes involved with some very dangerous people.